Artificial Intelligence at

Home

Will AI Help Us or Hurt Us?

Nick Hunter

T0112987

CHERITON

CHILDREN'S BOOKS

Published in 2025 by **Cheriton Children's Books**
1 Bank Drive West, Shrewsbury, Shropshire, SY3 9DJ, UK

© 2025 Cheriton Children's Books

First Edition

Author: Nick Hunter
Designers: Paul Myerscough and Jessica Moon
Editor: Sarah Eason
Proofreader: Kate Hobson

Picture credits: Cover: Shutterstock/Aslysun (foreground), Shutterstock/Gorodenkoff (bottom), Shutterstock/Piotr Wawrzyniuk (background); Inside: Throughout: Shutterstock/Nadya Art, p1: Shutterstock/Josep Suria, p5b: Shutterstock/PopTika, p5t: Shutterstock/Igor Rain, p6: Shutterstock/GrandeDuc, p7: Shutterstock/Creative Rabbit Hole, p8: Shutterstock, p9: Shutterstock/Fizkes, p10: Shutterstock/Rawpixel.com, p11: Shutterstock/Metamorworks, p12: Shutterstock, p13: Shutterstock/Gorodenkoff, p14: Shutterstock/Andrey Popov, p15: Shutterstock/RossHelen, p18: Shutterstock/Creative Shorts, p19: Shutterstock/PaO STUDIO, p20: Shutterstock/Inside Creative House, p21: Shutterstock/MikeDotta, p22: Roboat/MIT/AMS Institute, p23: Shutterstock/Dima Zel, p26: Shutterstock/Sergey Nivens, p27: Shutterstock/Josep Suria, p28: Shutterstock/MDV Edwards, p29: Shutterstock/Igor Link, p32: Shutterstock/Antoniodiaz, p33: Shutterstock/Gorodenkoff, p34: Shutterstock/Jacob Lund, p35: Shutterstock/Gorodenkoff, p36: Shutterstock/PeopleImages.com/Yuri A, p37: Shutterstock/Gorodenkoff, p41: Shutterstock/Zapp2Photo, p44: Shutterstock/PeopleImages.com/Yuri A, p47: Shutterstock/TippaPatt.

All rights reserved. No part of this book may be reproduced in any form without permission from the publisher, except by a reviewer.

Printed in China

Please visit our website,
www.cheritonchildrensbooks.com
to see more of our high-quality books.

Contents

What Is Artificial Intelligence?

Are you an expert in **artificial** intelligence (AI)? You may not think so but your family may use AI every day. When your phone can recognize your face to unlock itself, you're using AI. If you have a voice-controlled assistant or smart speaker at home that you can ask to play music or turn on the light, that's using AI to recognize your voice and process what you say. It seems to be thinking for us, but AI's use of data means it can follow our instructions instantly.

HOW DO WE DEFINE AI?

Before we look at the many changes it could bring to our homes, we need to consider what we mean by AI. Artificial intelligence describes the way that **software** or machines can be designed and programmed to do things that can normally be carried out only by intelligent beings, including humans. These things could include recognizing human speech, making complex decisions, and then also carrying out complex tasks based on the decisions that were made.

SMART THINKING

Even the simplest tasks you do every day require a large amount of data and complex intelligence. When you wake up in the morning, your brain recognizes an alarm or light through the window as a sign that it is time to wake up. Your brain then sends a message to your body to start the complex series of movements that take you from lying in bed to standing up. For a computer to copy this natural process, complex instructions and a lot of data are required. This data helps a computer respond as we would. When advanced computers are able to master human processes, it can have a powerful impact on the world and our place in it.

AI AND ROBOTS

In the near future, AI could control robots to help us in our homes. A **robot** is a machine that can carry out complex tasks automatically, sometimes by moving around. Robots can be controlled by powerful AI to function **autonomously**, without direct human control. However, other robots do not use AI because they might be programmed to do a specific task, such as cutting the grass or cleaning the floor.

Facial recognition works by comparing an image of your face to a stored map to match patterns between the two. AI could use such technology to operate systems in our homes.

THE BENEFITS AND THE RISKS

Since the beginning of the twenty-first century, there have been huge steps forward in the development of AI. Many people believe that the changes brought by this technology are just beginning and will affect all areas of our lives. A large number of those changes could be seen in our homes, from the way we cook our food to the way that we entertain ourselves, and far more. AI will bring major changes to the way we live and work. This will bring benefits but could also bring risks and problems for many people.

This book will look at how AI could change our homes and **debate** whether this new technology is our friend or **foe**. Look for **IS AI A FRIEND OR FOE?** throughout the book. Read the arguments for and against AI, then answer questions that invite you to draw your own conclusions about whether this transformative technology will help us or hurt us.

CHAPTER 1

The History of AI in the Home

The first modern computers were built in the 1950s. These were far more basic than today's computers and could fill an entire room. Early computer **pioneers** imagined a time when computers could think like humans. They realized that would need big changes in technology to create computers powerful enough to imitate human ways of thinking.

FROM FANTASY TO REALITY

AI was featured in movies and science-fiction stories long before it became a reality. The creators of these movies and books also wondered whether AI would be a good or bad thing for humans. Today, many people are asking these questions in real life.

For many years, developments in AI were slowed because computers were not powerful enough to process all the data required for AI. In 1997, there was a breakthrough when a computer called Deep Blue defeated world champion Garry Kasparov at chess. This showed that, in the controlled environment of a game with clear rules, a computer could think like a human and even be more effective at solving problems.

THE INTERNET OF MANY THINGS

The **Internet of Things (IoT)** was another idea that people started to talk about in the 1990s. This was based on the idea that home appliances could send and receive information over the Internet.

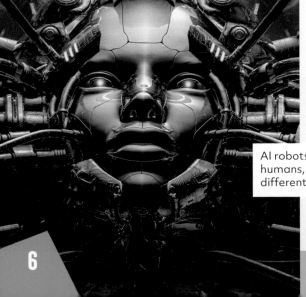

AI robots in movies often look like humans, but the reality is very different. AI is not humanlike.

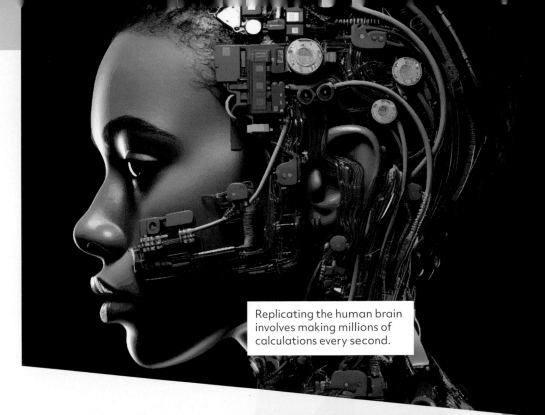

Replicating the human brain involves making millions of calculations every second.

One of the first IoT devices was a toaster connected to the Internet. Wireless Internet and **Bluetooth** made it easier to link different devices together. In the future, people planned that AI would be able to control these different devices just as well as humans.

ONLINE SEARCH

Basic forms of AI are familiar to us when we browse the Internet. For example, shopping websites make suggestions about what you might want to buy based on what you've bought before. Social media and search engines will use **algorithms** based on your personal data to present you with content and advertising that will fit best with your particular interests.

Enabling AI

Developments in AI depended on two things: the availability of large amounts of data including text and images for training AI systems, and powerful micro-processors **originally** designed for processing fast-moving graphics in gaming. These processors are capable of billions of calculations per second, which mean they appear to come up with answers or solutions almost instantly.

THINKING LIKE A HUMAN

Since 2000, developers have been able to use the vast range of data that we create on the Internet each day to train computers to **replicate** human thinking. In 2012, Google trained an AI system to recognize cats on a video. This was one of the first examples of a computer identifying detail in an image and paving the way for the facial recognition technology on many smartphones today. Developers created **neural networks** that use the structure of the human brain. This led to major advances in speech and image recognition.

Voice-activated assistants are a feature of many homes, but they will become more **sophisticated** than the devices we use today.

SPEAK TO YOUR ASSISTANT

In 2014, Amazon launched the Echo, often known as Alexa. This **voice-activated** assistant soon became popular and other technology companies launched their own versions. The voice-activated assistant brought AI into the average home. The success of these devices depended on being able to understand and respond to natural human language. They could be used to control other Internet-connected devices, for playing music and ordering products online. These voice-activated assistants were the first steps on the way to what were named "smart homes" with a lot of devices being controlled by AI.

As people rely more and more on home delivery services, AI will play a greater role in our lives at home. Could this present us with security concerns?

MAKING MISTAKES

However, voice-activated assistants also revealed some of the problems with AI in the home. Many people were concerned about privacy. The assistant listens to everything said in range of its microphone to detect its activation word such as "Alexa" or "Siri." Once activated, private conversations can be recorded. Many people are worried that their conversations are being recorded and stored on computers without permission. This data can then be used to advertise things to us or decide what we see on social media. There have also been examples of commands being misheard or mistakes being made as a result.

CHANGING THE WAY WE LIVE

Recent developments in AI have happened alongside many changes in the way we live. More people than ever before now work from home. Rather than going out to buy groceries and other goods, they are delivered to our homes. We communicate with our friends and watch movies and other entertainment online. All these changes mean that developments in AI will have a big impact in our homes. Are we ready for the enormous changes that AI will bring to our lives at home? Many people are ready to embrace the shift, but others are not so eager to do so.

CHAPTER 2

The Smart Home

Experts **predict** that our homes will become increasingly "smart." This means that we will rely on numerous Internet-connected devices as part of our daily lives. There are already millions of homes using some smart devices, such as TV and voice-activated assistants. However, the number of Internet-connected devices is growing quickly and can include heating controls, refrigerators, lighting, and many other appliances. Increasingly, these different appliances will be controlled by AI.

RECOGNIZING LANGUAGE

It is likely that voice-activated assistants will be at the heart of the smart home. Currently, these devices can perform relatively simple tasks such as searching for weather information or playing music. In the future, companies are looking to **integrate** more complex language models into their assistants. This will enable them to handle a wide range of different commands and requests, such as suggesting what you could cook and eat for dinner or finding a relaxing TV show for you to watch.

We use informal language when we talk to friends, which can be more difficult for AI to understand.

Your smart home could make sure a **driverless car** is ready to take you to school, the office, or anywhere else you need to be.

NO NEED TO TALK

As AI develops further, you may not need to speak to your assistant at all, because it will automatically activate based on your normal routine. For example, your helpful morning wake-up call could change depending on your daily schedule. Your AI assistant will also link to different devices such as kitchen robots to prepare meals.

INTELLIGENT ASSISTANT

AI will enable more powerful devices to learn about the people who live in the house and make changes without having to be told. It could track when you wake up in the morning, controlling the heat and lighting in the house and playing some of your favorite music. The assistant could also ensure that an AI-controlled driverless car is ready to take people to school or work.

How Does Natural Language Work?

Early examples of voice-activated assistants often made errors, confusing words that sound the same. AI systems are trained from millions of examples of texts and conversations. They can use their training to understand what you are likely to say so they are less likely to confuse words and so do the wrong thing. AI is also less likely to be confused by people speaking with unfamiliar accents.

HEALTHY FAMILY

As well as helping you prepare for the day ahead, your smart home could also keep a watch on your health. Cameras and sensors in your refrigerator can watch what you eat and suggest healthier options for breakfast. You could also be reminded to take medications or attend to other health needs. The home assistant could even link to wearable health devices such as smart watches to advise if you need more exercise or sleep.

A NEW AND DEEP UNDERSTANDING

Some companies are planning for your smart home to build a very deep understanding of your health and lifestyle. This could include monitoring the human waste you leave in the bathroom and advising what this could mean for your health and wellbeing.

PET CARE

It may not just be humans that can be kept healthy by AI. Pets can be given wearable devices that monitor their movement and health. The data can also tell if your dog or cat is overweight, as this is a major cause of many health conditions. Of course, cameras can also keep an eye on pets if the owner is out of the house and even talk to them to train the pet and be a good substitute for human company.

Wearable devices can measure your pet's health as well as your own.

12

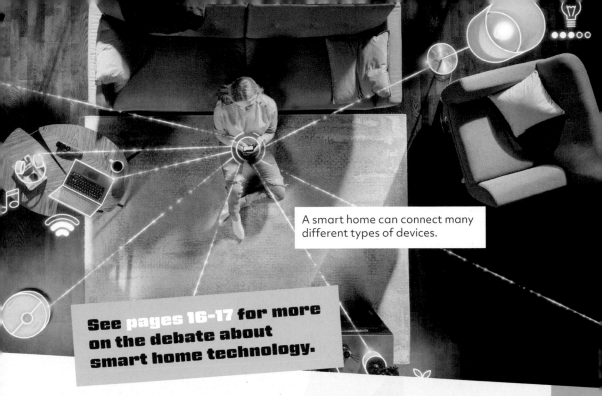

A smart home can connect many different types of devices.

See pages 16-17 for more on the debate about smart home technology.

HEALTHY HOME

AI tools in the smart home will also be able to check on the health of the home itself. As well as the temperature, sensors could also check on air quality and substances that might cause allergies. AI could also monitor the home's water supply and any problems that could require maintenance. All this would happen in the background, efficiently, and without human residents giving instructions.

BUILDING SMART HOMES

Will AI affect the way houses are built? We are used to new houses having pipes for running water, heating, and electrical wiring built into them. Builders are starting to build smart homes rather than adding technology later. AI tools could become like heating and wiring, built into a home from the outset, and we will be living in smart homes with inbuilt AI systems whether we like it or not.

ENVIRONMENTAL BENEFITS

Smart homes may make life easier for us, but they can also save energy and have environmental benefits too. AI can manage heating, lighting, and water use to ensure that energy is not wasted. AI will also open windows, close drapes, and shade windows to keep homes at an ideal temperature. AI could even be used to monitor how much carbon dioxide our homes release into the atmosphere, as this gas is one of the main causes of climate change.

AI can provide us with entertainment based on what we like, but to do this it uses a lot of different data about us.

SMART HOME PROBLEMS

Not everybody is looking forward to a future living in a smart home. Some people wonder whether we really need a smart assistant to open the drapes and dim the lights for us. If a computer is monitoring our health and telling us what we should eat, will this really make us healthier or better? Many people feel that all these things will just make life more complicated.

BLOCKING TECHNOLOGY

Technology could become such a big part of our daily lives that homes could also have technology-free rooms, which block wi-fi and Bluetooth signals. This is where we could go to escape the cameras, sensors, and microphones that would be monitoring every move.

USELESS WITHOUT AI SYSTEMS

Maybe we will all become so reliant on AI technology to run our lives that we are unable to make decisions for ourselves about our homes. It can be difficult to connect different devices so they work together correctly and AI could make this even more of a problem. One of the biggest worries about smart homes is the prospect of systems being **hacked** or infected with **malware**. Many people are very concerned about this issue. We will look at AI and security in more detail later in this book.

DATA AND PRIVACY

As with other areas of AI, having a fully connected smart home relies on a lot of data. AI tools use data to plan and make decisions, just as humans do. This data could include your daily schedule, banking details, or private health information. It is not always clear how AI systems use this data and what other systems they are shared with. As voice-activated assistants listen to everything we say, our private conversations may already be stored on a **server** somewhere.

LOSING PRIVACY

We have a right to privacy, but to make the best use of AI technology, we often must agree to technology businesses using and sharing this data. Often, we don't have a clear idea how this data is going to be used. People are concerned that this information could be used by governments to monitor their citizens or by businesses to target advertising. Some customers report that they have stopped using smart speakers because of their concerns about being targeted by advertisers.

Taking a break from technology can help us relax, along with protecting our privacy.

The Debate:

AI Will Make Our Homes More Comfortable

The promise of smart homes is that they will make our lives much easier, freeing us from the need to worry about everything from home entertainment to eating healthy food. Perhaps AI will take care of everything in our homes and make them more comfortable. There are arguments both for and against this scenario. Let's take a look.

AGREE

Time saving: Having home appliances and other systems controlled by AI will save us a lot of time, giving us more opportunities to relax and enjoy ourselves rather than thinking about chores or what we should cook and have for dinner.

Healthier environment: AI can monitor our own health but also our home environment to make sure the air is clean and alerting us to problems such as water leaks. This will make us healthier and more comfortable, which can only be beneficial to us.

AI will predict what we want: Over time, AI tools will learn how to control our homes with humans not needing to get involved in many decisions, such as controlling temperature or ordering food.

DISAGREE

System failures: Putting a lot of different devices together does not always work perfectly. The software in each device may not work with other devices. Ideas about perfect smart homes are based on the idea that devices work together and never break. The best AI tools for homes may be too expensive for most of us.

Privacy issues: To benefit from smart homes, we need to make a trade-off with AI technology. For computers to understand us and our needs, they need to collect a lot of data about us. This data may be stored on servers and accessed by other systems, and therefore could be accessed by many users, including criminals.

Losing control: If AI is controlling our homes, does that mean we don't have control? Losing control of the appliances in our homes will not make the home feel more comfortable, quite the opposite.

Conclusion

As with any technology that promises to change our lives, the results may not be what we expect. AI could make our homes more comfortable and efficient but we need to be wary of some of the negative aspects that could go alongside this, too.

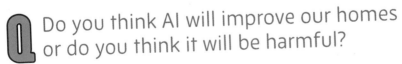

Do you think AI will improve our homes or do you think it will be harmful?

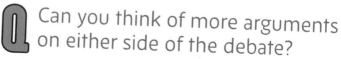

Can you think of more arguments on either side of the debate?

Will AI be a friend or a foe? What conclusions do you draw?

CHAPTER 3

The Personal Robot Revolution

If you think about AI helping in your home, you might picture a humanlike robot cooking your meals or cleaning the house. While robots will be part of the smart homes of the future, developers have many problems to solve before we start living with humanlike robots. Often, these challenges are physical rather than issues that AI can solve.

COPYING THE HUMAN BODY

Humanlike robots might not be doing our laundry any time soon because the human body is very difficult to replicate. AI can imitate natural human speech or recognize and copy particular elements in a picture, so it appears to think like a human. However, if you think about the range of things you can do with your hands, you will realize how incredibly complex your body is.

SO COMPLEX

Humans can hold a pen lightly and make the tiny movements needed to write things down. We can grip tightly to railings or steer a bicycle, but we can also pick up something fragile, such as an egg, without breaking it. Our brains are trained to recognize what to do by years of interaction with the world, and our bodies can follow the brain's instructions. It would take a huge amount of complex training for an AI robot to be able to do all this.

Robots will not need to look like humans to help us with everyday tasks, such as our office work and schoolwork.

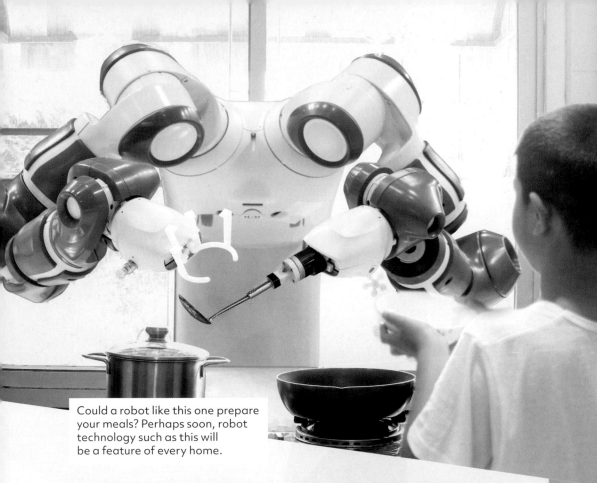

Could a robot like this one prepare your meals? Perhaps soon, robot technology such as this will be a feature of every home.

It would have to recognize fragile objects and adjust its grip instantly. Movement is another tricky area —it's much easier for a robot to **navigate** on wheels than on legs.

THE LIMITS OF ROBOTICS

Humanlike robots are limited in what they can do. Unless you have a vast house (and plenty of money), it's not really practical to have different robots for all the varied tasks you might want help with. Some homes now have robots that can vacuum the floor or cut the lawn. These robots are programmed for a particular task rather than requiring the problem-solving and planning abilities of a true AI robot.

ROBOTS IN THE KITCHEN

One area in which robots could become more common is in the kitchen. The robot could read a recipe, chop and mix ingredients, or cook ingredients that are already chopped. These robots could be particularly useful in busy professional kitchens but could also save time in the home. Imagine coming home to a robot that is already preparing your dinner!

ROBOTS THAT CARE

Robots may not be able to do all the practical things that humans can now, but can they provide humans with company and even care for **vulnerable** people? Social robots can use AI for a range of different uses. These may include looking after children by alerting a parent if the child leaves the room or does anything that could be dangerous or potentially harmful.

Social robots can also provide company and care for older people or anyone living alone. The robot can notify medical or emergency services if their human companion has an accident. This could help keep people safe and have similar benefits to an animal companion in helping tackle loneliness.

SOCIABLE ROBOTS?

There are many issues with the idea of social robots. Although the robot may be able to give a clear and convincing reply to anything we say, that does not mean it would be an effective replacement for human company. However intelligent the robot may appear, it is just a machine with software to copy what a human would do, so is not expressing real feelings. As people become used to communicating with AI, this may become less important, but may limit how much people use social robots.

A social robot could help older people keep safe in their homes. It may also become a companion, providing a solution to loneliness.

This robot is designed to interact and have conversations with humans. The screen also shows messages and information.

DESIGNING HOMES FOR ROBOTS

If mobile robots do become common, many homes will need to be redesigned. They will need to be suitable for wheels or whatever technology robots use to move. For example, robots may need wider doorways to navigate and any doors would need to open and close automatically. Steps and stairs could be a major obstacle for mobile robots. If your home is full of clutter, robots would have to deal effectively with that as well.

Developers may be able to find solutions to the problems of mobile robots, but there are still other issues to consider. Imagine you have a robot on wheels that tidies your bedroom, picking up all the clothes and other objects you leave on the floor as well as food wrappers and other trash. How does the robot know what to keep and what to throw out? What if you left something important on the floor that the robot didn't recognize? How would your teacher react if you said the robot threw out your homework? AI-controlled robots can identify different objects but this works better if objects are clearly packaged and labeled. That's not usually the way homes are arranged, so we may need to redesign our homes for AI to work.

Although not yet suitable for homes, some robotic navigation is effective. For example, Roboats are autonomous boats that travel on the many canals that run through Amsterdam in the Netherlands, Europe.

FOOD FAILURES

Using robots to prepare food could mean that a kitchen will have to be redesigned if the robot needs to collect ingredients from cupboards or a refrigerator. Will it be able to recognize different ingredients or would they need to be placed in a particular order, like goods in a warehouse? Food packaging is often difficult for humans to open. If you think about all the complications, you may wonder how much time the robot would save and whether it would really make life easier. A robot that could do all this would also be very sophisticated, with a very big price tag to match the elaborate idea.

MAINTAINING YOUR ROBOT

The more moving parts a robot has, the more likely it is to break down. Problems with AI software may be quite easy to fix, just by restarting the system or loading a software update. Fixing problems with cameras, wheels, or robot arms may be more difficult and involve calling an engineer. That could be costly and time-consuming, too.

DO WE NEED MOBILE ROBOTS?

Some experts have questioned whether the problems associated with autonomous mobile robots are actually worth solving for use at home. We can design robots for specific tasks or for working in very structured environments, such as moving objects around in warehouses. However, homes are all different and therefore more difficult to navigate. Engineers are working on mobile versions of voice-activated assistants. If these cannot do physical tasks, it might just be better and less expensive to have an assistant in every room rather than one that moves around.

FIXING PROBLEMS

Developers are undoubtedly working to solve some of the possible problems that may stop every home from having an autonomous robot controlled by AI. Robots can connect to online data to identify different objects that they have not encountered before. Technology such as sensors and motors will become more common, and so easier to fix and replace. Engineers are also working to make robots more mobile and have more skill in picking things up and moving them around. We already have autonomous robots that can operate in the deep ocean and on other planets, but human homes are one of the biggest challenges.

Scientists have developed robots that can operate on Mars, but there are fewer obstacles there than in a busy home on Earth.

The Debate:

Robots Will Run Our Homes

Movies and TV shows have made us familiar with the idea of robots that can help us with everyday tasks, although movie robots are rarely shown folding laundry or cleaning the bathroom. Some people predict that autonomous robots will soon be part of every smart home. Perhaps robots will soon run our homes and take over all our everyday tasks. There are arguments both for and against this scenario.

AGREE

Next logical step: Developers have created AI tools that can replicate many of the ways that humans think. Using AI to control autonomous robots that copy the way humans move must be the logical next step.

Robots are taking over many areas of work: More robots are being used in factories and warehouses, where they can do various jobs well. They should be able to do the same thing in homes. Many homes use robots for tasks such as vacuuming. These are not controlled by AI at present but this shows that robots are useful in the home.

We all want to save time and effort: Time is precious and devices that can save people time and give them more opportunities to do other things are likely to be popular with most people.

DISAGREE

Physical limitations: There are many issues with designing robots that can do a range of tasks at home as easily and effectively as humans can. Some of these limitations may be difficult to solve.

Cost and convenience: Sophisticated robots will be expensive and we may need multiple robots for different tasks. Many of us will not think it is worth paying the price for a robot servant.

Adjustments to homes: Our homes will have to be modified to enable robots to move around them, which will add extra cost and may not improve our living space, despite the expense.

Conclusion

At present, it is difficult to see robot servants becoming a feature of many homes because they are not **adaptable** enough to do many of the tasks that we need them to do. However, we will see more robots in other settings and they may eventually become a common part of home life.

Do you think robots could run our homes or do you think that is impractical and even harmful?

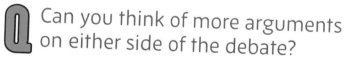
Can you think of more arguments on either side of the debate?

Will AI be a friend or a foe? What conclusions do you draw?

CHAPTER 4

Home Security

One main feature of the smart home will be AI-controlled security gadgets. A reason for this is that the more our homes know about us and what we need, the more opportunities there are for criminals. In the past, criminals could only enter the house through an unlocked door or window. Today, they can use Internet-connected devices to commit crimes.

BIOMETRIC TECHNOLOGY

AI could spell the end for the front door key as the locks on our homes will be increasingly linked to **biometric** technology. Cameras will recognize our faces or we will scan hand or fingerprints to get into the house. AI will also give us more access to security devices such as cameras and sensors, which will be able to monitor any movements. Facial recognition software will help in identifying any intruders that appear on cameras. This could be particularly useful in large apartment blocks in which hundreds of people could walk in and out every day.

Cameras and other sensors inside the house will offer another level of security to identify intruders. These cameras and sensors can be monitored by AI and sound the alarm by contacting police or other security operators if needed.

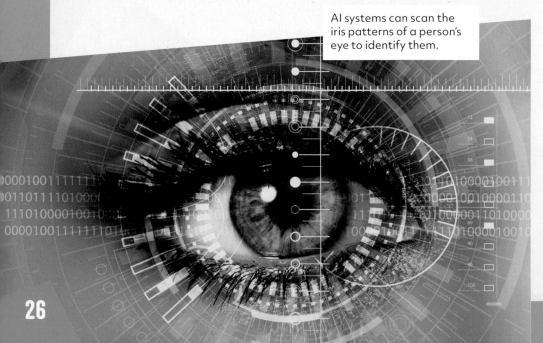

AI systems can scan the iris patterns of a person's eye to identify them.

Some people warn that when more of our lives are controlled by digital systems, we will be more vulnerable to **hackers**.

CRIMINALS AND AI

AI can increase the security of our homes, but there is another side to this story. Criminals also have access to AI and this will give these people a lot of new weapons as they try to trick and steal from us. If the locks on our doors are controlled by AI, they may be more secure and convenient for us, but they may be possible to open remotely. Unfortunately, the cameras that monitor homes can help a hacker monitor them too.

HACKING SMART HOMES

The number of connected devices in a smart home network can also be a target for computer hackers. Anything that connects to the Internet can be hacked. In a smart home this could include devices such as cameras, smart appliances, or even lights. Hackers could use cameras to see whether anyone is in the house or to spy on the home. They could also use these appliances to send malware to the home network and access computers containing private information about the owners.

PROTECTING OUR HOMES

AI tools can help protect homes from hackers. AI can constantly scan all files and data to detect threats much more quickly than was possible in the past. AI systems can also act to remove or defend against these threats and protect important data from any breaches.

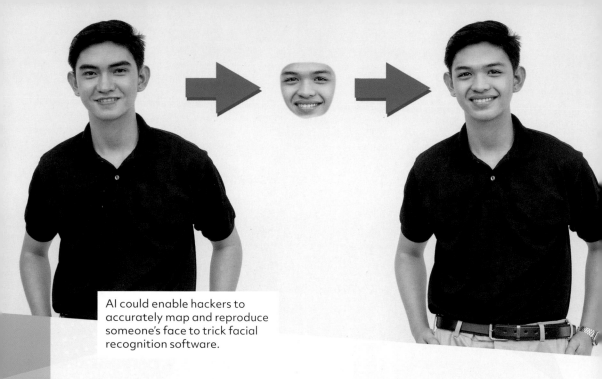

AI could enable hackers to accurately map and reproduce someone's face to trick facial recognition software.

HELPING THE HACKERS

The main problem with AI and home security is that hackers are also using AI. For example, AI can make it much easier to crack passwords. Criminals can also use AI to launch a huge number of attacks or malware files very quickly. One of the risks is that AI can manage very large networks of interconnected devices, with little human input. This means that if hackers are able to trick or bypass AI controls, they can affect many devices at once and cause serious problems for networks.

PERSONAL SAFETY

We don't just need to think about the devices and systems in our homes. Keeping online profiles and files safe can be just as important as protecting your home. Some criminals try to target us in our own homes by trying to disrupt our online lives. AI offers new ways for them to target people.

TRICKS AND SCAMS

Phishing is a type of **scam** in which criminals use emails, messages, or phone calls to trick their victims. They typically try to persuade victims to give details of bank accounts or credit cards, or to send them money directly. **Generative AI** can be used to create text and images that are almost identical to examples that already exist. Criminals could make these scams far more convincing by using Generative AI to create incredibly convincing text and images that are very difficult for people to spot as fakes.

SOCIAL MEDIA

People who use any form of social media, such as Snapchat, TikTok, or Instagram, need to be aware that text, pictures, and videos may not always be what they seem. Deepfake media can be created by people using AI to mislead us, or to trick us, into revealing personal details online. While AI can help identify these deepfakes, we also need to think for ourselves. If something does not seem real, think about the source and whether it's reliable. You should always discuss anything that makes you uncomfortable with a trusted adult.

Deepfake technology could be used to replace one person's face with another, and make it almost undetectable.

What Is a Deepfake?

Deepfakes are images, video, or other media created using an AI process called deep learning. These images show fake events or people saying things that they have never said. They are made by training an AI system with thousands of images of one person or one event until the AI can recreate it. Voices can also be copied in this way. Some deepfakes are created for entertainment but there are concerns that many will be created to mislead or attack individuals.

The Debate:

AI Will Make Our Homes More Secure

One of the key functions of any home is that it should be a secure place to live. Perhaps the features of AI systems such as cameras will make our homes safer places in which to live. There are arguments both for and against this scenario. Let's take a look.

AGREE

Safe locks: Open or insecure locks are one of the main ways criminals can access buildings. AI's use of biometric technology will give us more ways to keep our homes secure, and ensure that we can't leave doors unlocked. Many people will benefit from that extra level of security, particularly those who are busy or perhaps less conscious about checking their home security.

Recognizing intruders: AI systems will use cameras and sensors to recognize who belongs in the house and raise the alarm if cameras pick up anything unusual. That will be reassuring to many people, perhaps particularly those who live alone.

Combating hackers: Devices in our smart homes will be tempting to hackers, but AI will be a key weapon in identifying **cybercrime** and dealing with it quickly. AI will provide us with vital security.

DISAGREE

Smart homes help hackers: Hackers and criminals have access to AI as well and can use this to create new threats to the devices in smart homes. This will introduce a new area of danger at home.

Human error: Many online crimes rely on humans being tricked by email or other scams and sharing personal information. AI won't help us to be smarter about spotting criminals.

Deepfake images: Deepfake imagery and other media created by AI will be more realistic than ever before, so we will need to find ways of spotting them to make sure we are not misled.

Conclusion

AI will give us tools to make our homes safer but will also mean we have more attempted crimes to deal with online. The most important thing is to be on our guard and follow the same safety rules we do now, such as not giving our personal information to strangers.

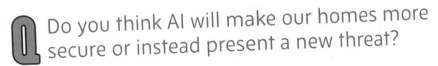

Q Do you think AI will make our homes more secure or instead present a new threat?

Q Can you think of more arguments on either side of the debate?

Q Will AI be a friend or a foe? What conclusions do you draw?

CHAPTER 5

Leisure Time and Family Life

Supporters of AI tell us that it will make our lives easier. It will help with chores at home and support us at school. Workers will have more time to relax as AI will take over part of everyone's jobs. Some people even predict that we won't need to work at all. If this is true, how will AI help us enjoy our leisure time and family life?

KEEPING US ENTERTAINED

One of the first areas of life to be affected by AI was home entertainment. Entertainment companies such as Netflix and YouTube use all the data they have about what you like to watch to create algorithms that make recommendations for what you might like to watch in the future.

FROM SIMPLE TO COMPLEX

At first, algorithms were quite basic in what they recommended, for example, if you like comedy, a list of different comedies were recommended. Now, the recommendations for videos, movies, or music we might like are much more **personalized**, and this trend will continue as AI improves. With so much choice today, AI-powered searches that can take us directly to the media we want could save us valuable time.

Social media use AI to keep us browsing and scrolling for as long as possible.

See pages 38-39 for more on the debate about AI and family life.

Have you ever loved a TV series so much that you felt like it was created just for you? Perhaps that will start to happen more often as AI technology becomes more sophisticated.

BIG BUSINESS

Having the best recommendation system is big business. The social media company Meta owns Facebook and Instagram, both of which have hundreds of millions of registered users. They want their users to spend as much time as possible on their favorite social media site or app. Meta says that it is using huge amounts of data to improve its recommendations, and AI tools work with this data to get a clear picture of what users want.

WILL WE BE CONTROLLED?

As the algorithms that decide what content we see online use more and more data and complex AI, only a few people will really understand how they work. They will show us content that is closely matched to what we've watched before, who our friends are, and the detail of our social media profiles. However, we will not know what we are missing or not being shown. We could be only seeing one side of an argument or missing out on important knowledge.

CREATING ENTERTAINMENT

AI could even start to create videos or TV shows especially for us. We know that AI can create deepfake images and videos based on things that already exist. Maybe AI could create new videos or music based on our favorite characters or artists.

INTERACTIVE GAMING

Gaming is another area of home entertainment that will see big changes because of AI. We know that AI can learn to talk and act like a human, and this can bring video game characters to life so nonplayable characters (NPCs) and opponents can start to behave and interact like other players. These characters will seem as though they are alive.

LIVING ONLINE

Games will become more interactive and exciting than ever. In the future, AI may be able to recreate realistic game worlds so games can keep reinventing themselves. Virtual reality (VR) worlds already exist but these could become ever-more realistic, tempting us to spend more and more of our time playing games.

GAMING DRAWBACKS

There are drawbacks to these exciting AI developments. We know that too much gaming is not good for us. It can affect our ability to get as much sleep as we need. When we're gaming, we're also not physically active and this may lead to problems such as gaining weight and back pain. In extreme cases, gamers become addicted. Gaming can also affect our social skills and ability to interact with others.

KEEPING FIT

While AI may make some of us less active, we can use AI to help us take more exercise too. Smart watches, fitness trackers, and other devices already collect data about our health and how much exercise we take.

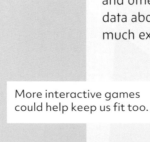

More interactive games could help keep us fit too.

Home gyms are already a reality. AI and VR could help us get truly **immersed** in sports without ever leaving home.

Smart home gyms use AI to create customized workouts and give advice on fitness, and three-dimensional (3-D) sensors detect how your body is moving and give personalized guidance.

CREATING A PLAN
Generative AI tools such as OpenAI's ChatGPT can help us to work on our fitness. These tools can **generate** new text such as reports and other documents. If you ask ChatGPT to produce a fitness or workout plan for a particular purpose, such as losing weight or building strength, AI will learn from all the different examples of fitness plans used in its training to provide a useful workout plan.

A FITNESS FIRST
These changes could be a big deal for the fitness industry. If we can exercise at home and build our own online training programs, there may be less need for people to take out expensive gym memberships or pay for advice and help from equally expensive personal trainers.

CHANGING FAMILY LIFE

If AI enables us all to live in our own personal bubble, this could change family life as we know it. Many of us already spend more time than we should looking at individual screens rather than spending family time together. AI could increase this as it makes the world more personal to each individual. AI can use data about what we do, where we go, and who we communicate with to know more about each of us. This could mean that we are happy for AI tools to decide how we spend our leisure time, but this is unlikely to be a good thing for our personal relationships.

If we're all constantly immersed in VR, that could have an impact on family life. Would that be a good thing? Perhaps it would be **detrimental** to our relationships.

TECH-FREE TIME

One way to deal with the risk posed by AI is to make sure that we all set aside times when we are not using AI and other technology. This is almost certainly good for our mental health as well as our relationships with family and friends. We could set aside AI-free mealtimes or times of the week when we have a break from our **AI-enabled** world. Making sure we set aside time for outdoor exercise will also benefit our physical health.

SENSE OF PURPOSE

One of the biggest fears about the growth of AI is that it will involve many people losing their jobs as AI takes over many areas of work. These changes could cause disruption for many families if new jobs are not created to replace those taken by AI. However, some people worry that the way we relate to work and leisure will change if AI is able to do so many tasks at home and in the workplace. If we are not needed to carry out chores at home, will this have a deeper impact on our wellbeing? Lack of work could be very difficult for many people to deal with.

ENJOYING LIFE

Some people question whether they want to allow AI to take over so many areas of our lives. It may be a cool idea for a robot to cook our meals sometimes, but for many of us, cooking and eating a meal together is a great pleasure. AI may enable us to live much of our life without leaving the house, but we would miss out on time with friends, meeting new people, and enjoying nature, which can be some of the great pleasures of life.

Simulating worlds and experiences may not be as exciting as the real world.

The Debate:

AI Will Improve Family Life

Often one of the biggest problems for families is to find time to do things together as everyone is generally very busy with work, school, and other activities. There are also all the chores to do at home. Perhaps AI will free up more time for families to spend together and thereby improve family life. There are arguments both for and against this scenario. Let's take a look at some of them.

AGREE

More leisure time: Experts predict that AI will take over many tasks at work and this will mean there is more leisure time for most people. Some people think this will be great for everyone.

Fewer chores: Smart homes are designed to reduce the time we need to spend doing chores. If this is the case, families will have more time to spend together and enjoy each other's company.

Improved home entertainment and fitness: AI will give us access to new advances in home entertainment and gaming, and will also be able to support us in keeping fit, which will improve our health.

DISAGREE

Personal worlds: Improvements in entertainment and gaming will make them more personal to each of us. This could have the effect of isolating us from people around us, including our family members. Many people believe this will be detrimental.

Job losses: Job changes may mean people have more time on their hands, but will they be able to enjoy it? Work not only allows us to earn the money we need to live, it also gives a purpose in life for many people. Too much leisure may not make us happy.

Too much AI: Many people worry that AI could take over too much of our lives and take away many things that we enjoy doing.

Conclusion

AI could give us more leisure time, so it could be a good thing for families. However, there is the risk that the opportunities of AI take over too much of our lives and we don't have enough time for other people. It is also likely that the benefits of AI at home will be uneven, only available to those who can afford them.

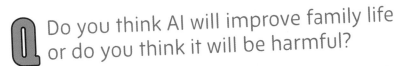
Q Do you think AI will improve family life or do you think it will be harmful?

Q Can you think of more arguments on either side of the debate?

Q Will AI be a friend or a foe? What conclusions do you draw?

CHAPTER 6

Friend or Foe?

AI has already played a part in changing our homes in many ways. Voice-activated assistants that can carry out tasks and facial recognition technology were the stuff of science fiction just a few years ago. Now, they are part of many people's lives. AI technology is developing so fast that the changes it will bring are difficult to predict. In the long term, AI could make our home lives very different. There will be winners and losers from the AI revolution.

WHO WILL BE THE WINNERS?

Many of us will benefit from the convenience that AI-controlled smart devices will bring at home. This could be because robots are able to help us with household chores or AI gives us access to home entertainment. There may also be some downsides to these changes, such as becoming too reliant on AI in our lives.

The businesses that develop the devices and AI technology for smart homes will be big winners from the growth of AI as this will enable the development of a wide range of new technology. Smart homes will also provide many different businesses with a lot more data about all of us and how we live. This will direct the creation of new cutting-edge AI tools.

Smart home technology will also give new opportunities to cybercriminals using AI to commit crimes and target the devices in our homes. AI tools will be an important weapon in the fight against these criminals.

WHO WILL BE THE LOSERS?

The AI revolution will not benefit everyone equally and there will certainly be losers. While homes in developed countries may benefit more from AI technology, these benefits may not be shared around the world or even in poorer communities in developed countries. This unequal situation could be worsened by job losses in many industries that could increase gaps between rich and poor.

Even those people who are able to enjoy the benefits of smart homes may also see some changes that are less positive.

For example, reliance on AI could give us too much leisure time, which may not be good for everyone. There is also the worry that if family members let AI control their lives, this could be bad for family life and personal wellbeing.

AI can bring benefits to all of us, but there are also risks. If AI becomes too powerful, it could make our lives worse rather than better.

Rather than appearing as a robot, AI could become such a hidden part of our homes that we barely notice it, except perhaps when it stops working!

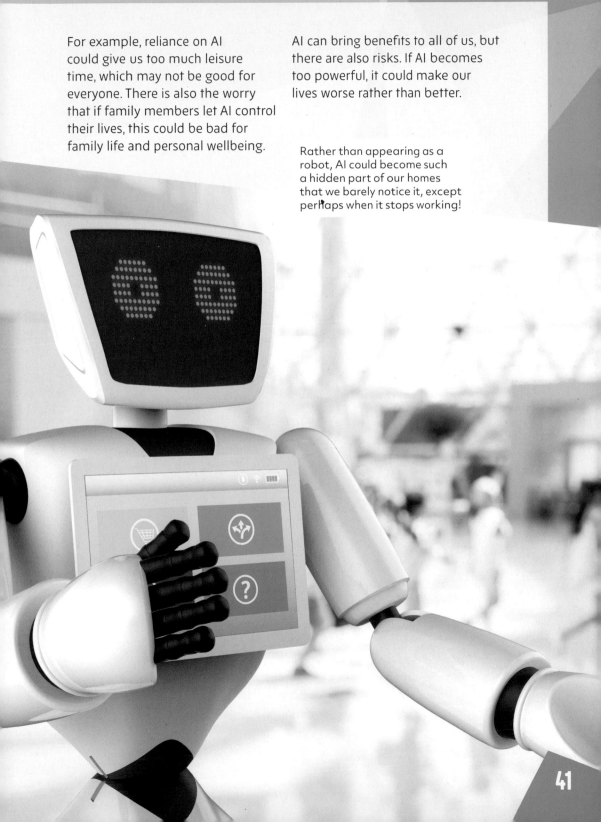

The Debate:

AI in Homes Will Make the World a Better Place

Smart homes controlled by AI may make life easier for many people, and perhaps the benefits of AI at home will make people everywhere healthier and be beneficial to the wider world. There are arguments both for and against this scenario. Let's take a look at some of them.

AGREE

Balance between work and leisure: AI promises to take over more of the tasks we prefer not to do and give us more time to enjoy ourselves. This should particularly benefit women, who do more household chores than men according to research.

Environmental benefits: Smart homes can reduce carbon dioxide emissions that cause climate change by controlling how homes use energy. That will be beneficial to people and the environment.

Health benefits: AI can help us to make healthier choices in our lifestyle, such as eating the right food and taking more exercise. Many people struggle to make healthy choices, or do not have the time to ensure they are making sensible decisions about their health. Having the support of AI to make informed and careful decisions will benefit a lot of people and keep them healthier.

DISAGREE

Not everyone will benefit: The benefits of AI in the home are most likely to be felt by homeowners in wealthier countries who are able to spend money on smart homes and beneficial AI tools.

Effect on families: While we may have more leisure time, we could be spending more time using AI for games and home entertainment than we spend with family or exploring the world, which could detrimentally affect our mental and physical health.

Disruption for workers: There are many predictions that AI will disrupt a lot of industries and this may lead to unemployment as people adjust to this new world. This loss of jobs and direction could be bad for the people affected and for society in general.

Loss of privacy: AI depends on a lot of data and information to be effective. This could mean loss of privacy for all of us as our data is shared. Are we really happy to pay this heavy price?

Conclusion

Much of the debate about whether AI in the home is a good thing depends on whether this technology is available to everyone. This is difficult to predict. There is certainly much to carefully consider if all the issues around AI are to be solved.

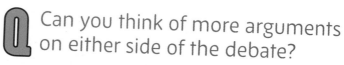 Do you think AI will improve our world or do you think it will harm it?

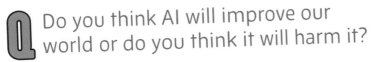 Can you think of more arguments on either side of the debate?

 Will AI be a friend or a foe? What conclusions do you draw?

The Ethics of AI

AI could have far-reaching effects on our home life, and raises a lot of **ethical** questions for developers and governments, and for all of us who use AI. Rules about the future of AI need to cover some of the areas outlined below.

- Privacy: Our homes are private places but AI will collect a lot of data about what we do and say. How do we know that this data will be used fairly?
- Control and transparency: AI may make our lives more convenient but are we in control of our smart homes? If we don't know the details of how AI tools work, how can we be sure that AI is making the right decisions for us?

- Health and wellbeing: If we rely too much on AI, could that affect our physical and mental health? As a society, we should investigate these effects, and what should we do if we discover that AI is actually bad for us?

AI could also lead to more unequal societies. The benefits of smart homes will be available to those who can afford them, but will they truly benefit everyone in society?

Q What rules would you put in place to ensure that AI will benefit the widest number of people?

Q Are there other ethical issues that you think should be considered?

Find Out More

BOOKS

Enz, Tammy. *Artificial Intelligence at Home and on the Go: 4D An Augmented Reading Experience* (The World of Artificial Intelligence 4D). Capstone, 2019.

Gitlin, Martin. *Smart Homes* (21st Century Skills Innovation Library: Exploring the Internet of Things). Cherry Lake, 2020.

Sonneborn, Liz. *Robots at Home* (Searchlight Books—Exploring Robotics). Lerner Publishing Group, 2023.

ONLINE

Visit McKinsey for Kids: Game on! to discover why your computer learns faster and games better than you think:
www.mckinsey.com/featured-insights/mckinsey-for-kids/ game-on-why-your-computer-learns-faster-and-games- better-than-you-think

Watch this video and discover how AIs such as ChatGPT learn:
https://youtu.be/R9OHn5ZF4Uo

Watch this CNBC video clip to discover how smart homes of the future are connecting more than 150 devices:
https://youtube.com/watch?v=UcCH_8TaGtk

To find out more about AI you can also search for websites of companies involved in AI such as OpenAI, the creator of ChatGPT, and Google's DeepMind.

Publisher's note to educators and parents:
All the websites featured above have been carefully reviewed to ensure that they are suitable for students. However, many websites change often, and we cannot guarantee that a site's future contents will continue to meet our high standards of educational value. Please be advised that students should be closely monitored whenever they access the Internet.

Glossary

adaptable can be changed or made useful for a different purpose

AI-enabled helped by AI

algorithms processes or sets of rules to be followed for a computer to solve a problem or perform a task

artificial describes something made by humans and not naturally occurring

autonomously working on its own without human control

biometric biological data such as fingerprints or facial characteristics

Bluetooth short-range technology for exchanging data between devices over a short distance

cybercrime crime committed using computers and the Internet

debate an argument or discussion about a particular subject, in which arguments are given for and against the main question

detrimental harmful

driverless car an autonomous car that does not need a human driver to operate it

ethical relating to moral rules that decide how people behave

facial recognition describing software that can recognize faces of individuals, such as when the user's face unlocks a smartphone

foe an enemy

generate to create

generative AI software that can create new content such as documents or images using AI

hacked a computer system that has been broken into

hackers people who break into computer systems

immersed deeply involved in something

integrate to combine or connect to work together

Internet of Things (IoT) a network of devices such as household appliances that share data with each other

malware software that is designed to disrupt or damage a computer system

navigate to determine a location and plan directions, or find the way around a system

neural networks networks that operate like the human brain with very complex connections

originally first made or seen

personalized designed or changed to meet individual needs

phishing fraudulently sending emails or other messages for financial or personal gain

pioneers the first people to do something

predict to say what will happen in the future

replicate to copy or reproduce

robot a machine that is able to replicate human functions or movements automatically

scam a trick designed to mislead others, particularly using computers or the Internet

server a computer used for storing data as part of a network

simulating imitating something that is real

software programs or instructions that affect how a computer operates

sophisticated highly complex

voice-activated can recognize and respond to the human voice

vulnerable can be easily attacked

Index

About the Author

Nick Hunter is a highly experienced children's book author, who has written countless titles on many subjects, from history and science through social studies and geography. In writing this book he has discovered that AI is an incredibly powerful technology that has the potential to bring great benefits to our homes if we manage its potential risks.